Cry, Howl

In Praise of
Cry, Howl

Edward Vidaurre - A STUNNING POET OF MAGNIFICENT HUMANITY! His poems take my breath away.

— **Naomi Shihab Nye**, Award-winning Palestinian-American Poet, Essayist & Educator

El poemario *Cry, Howl* de Edward Vidaurre es una colección de poemas incisivos que penetran la realidad perturbante de una metrópolis que asedia al ser en su más frágil definición: la apoteósis de una ciudad degolladora. El poeta se arma de imágenes poderosas que estructuran la ciudad ahogante que a todos nos habita. La familia y la relatividad emocional de los seres queridos vienen a ser la tabla salvadora que nos rescata de nuestro propio precipicio. Existe un tejer y entretejer de axiomas infinitos en esta poesía de Vidaurre que la valida como poesía portentosa, poesía que se nos queda grabada en lo más recóndito de nuestro ser.

— **Benito Pastoriza Iyodo**, author of *Hominis Aurora and September Elegies*

Edward Vidaurre's *Cry, Howl* takes the bus ride, the workday, the minutes of a life and sees them through the eyes of poetry. *"Algunos niños tienen el pueblo en sus ojos,"* Vidaurre writes, and his work gifts us that kind of vision. In the midst of strife and chaos and a pandemic and the day's politics, this collection offers a benediction through its words, *"Where they land/May they heal...May they heal/Wherever they may land"*

— **ire'ne lara silva**, author of *Cuicacalli/House of Song*

Unforgettable and moving, Edward Vidaurre's *Cry, Howl* will transport you to a new place. You will learn that sometimes you have to peer into the abyss to become human again. After reading this book, you will not be the same.

— **William W. Sokoloff**, author of *"Edward Vidaurre and the Politics of the Cholo Strut"* & *Political Science Pedagogy A Critical, Radical and Utopian Perspective*

also by Edward Vidaurre

Pandemia & Other Poems
JAZzHOUSE
Ramona and rumi: Love in the Time of Oligarchy: & unedited
Necessary Poems
Chicano Blood Transfusion
Beautiful Scars: Elegiac Beat Poems
Insomnia
I Took My Barrio On A Road Trip

Cry, Howl

poems by

Edward Vidaurre

PRICKLY PEAR PUBLISHING
& NOPALLI PRESS

Prickly Pear Publishing
Copyright © 2022 by Edward Vidaurre
ISBN: 978-1-889568-09-6
Library of Congress Control Number: 2022930009
First Edition, 2022

Published by Prickly Pear Publishing
in the United States of America.
www.pricklypearpublishing.com

Cover photography by Edward Vidaurre
Translations by Edward Vidaurre and Gabriella Gutiérrez y Muhs

Cover Art Design by Edward Vidaurre
Set in Adobe Garamond Pro

PRICKLY PEAR PUBLISHING
& NOPALLI PRESS

— *for the trees*

Contents

I. CRY

II. HOWL

I. CRY

"There are places we fear, places we dream, places whose exiles we became and never learned it until, sometimes, too late."

— **Thomas Pynchon**

Reading on the RTD, 1991-1993

Before I had a car
I read on the bus to and from work
I read Black Boy and Native Son
I read Invisible Man and Always Running
I read Dostoyevsky and some Langston Hughes
I read the L.A. Times and the Herald Examiner
I read many books and magazines
But mostly, I read the graffiti on the bus
& the faces of the beat, of the nervous
I read the lines on their hands & scars on their faces
I read the abuse and hungry and scared
I read the beauty on the eyeshadow and contour
on womens faces, the miles on their heels
I read the eyes of the drunk and heartbroken
I read their shoes for their travels and aches
I read their breath, the long sighs and whispers
I read on the RTD bus line
& now... I will write about it.

Robbed at Knife-Point

The bus ride was bumpy and too fast,
it was definitely a weekday
I always walked to the back of the bus,
window seat facing the right side
where I could see the people get on and off

I could see the gutters, the businesses opening up early,
the drama of the day unfolding, lovers holding hands, stray dogs
panting and rummaging through trash, the homelessness of my city
extending their hands, my view was of the grind, la lucha.
I carried a backpack with books, cassette tapes,
and markers for taggin' even though
I sucked at it and had given up on it
several years back, It was a constant for me

That day I jumped on the bus on 7th & Spring,
I remember I was listening to some Roger & Zapp,
I was a bit tired from the double shift
I worked the day before. Between songs and reading
from Rodriguez' "Always Running" I heard voices,

grunts, and the sound of people pushing against
each other as the bus filled up. I scooted my body
and leaned my head on the graffiti marked window,
then dozed off.

My eyes opened up a bit later to see a short,
long-haired kid, white t-shirt, and dickies pants,
Nike shoes, pinche cholo cagao'
I dressed the same in my barrio.

He kept looking around, hands in pockets
as if he were cold. The bus came to a stop
near McArthur Park, want to see a melting pot?

6

If you didn't get shot, stabbed, or drowned in
the lake there, you were fortunate. That day
I got robbed at knife-point.

This is what I remember: The bus stopped, people were getting
on and off and this kid in his teens pulled out a knife and stuck it
to my neck with one hand while he took my watch and backpack,
with the other, jumped off the bus and walked away.

The bus driver never saw it, and no one made a commotion,
I looked at him run away with my bag, inside
the pages of Ellison and Villaseñor
became instant orphans.

The bus slowly pulled away,
I stared at the lake, a lone swan sat on its murky waters,
I hadn't seen a swan so beautiful as that one, and haven't since.

Cry, Howl

I

In your morning fog
yawning at daybreak

I feel your
suck and moan
in letters

Steal me an avocado
from the grocery store
or ask father
he gives them away for free

Cry
when she cries
when she cries
Cry

Howl
as you die
as you die
Howl

Cry
for my city
running on warning
& low wattage
on low wages
& melting asphalt

Howl
In your pastel
queer dreams

& flip flops
from the top
of the stairs
& heroin blasted toes

Cry, Howl
On Juneteenth
for the real beat lyrics
of Amiri, Kaufman, & LeRoi

Cry, Howl
the disappearance of
privilege and the ugly squads
the sinking
of ships carrying
Conservative literature
printed in China
for the hypocrisy

Cry
when she cries
when she cries
Cry

Howl
as you die
as you die
Howl

Cry, Howl
for Lawrence
& Jim Morrison
& Robert & Bob
& Roque & Francisco
for the new strain
for the math in pandemia

To our dead
For you we cry
For you we howl
For you we drink
For you we eat
For you we kill
For you we harvest
For you we work
For you we develop

Howl
here come the UFOs
here come the blamed
here come the white teeth
Nothing has changed
The avocado seed sprouts a root

Howl
like the quarantine dogs
the shuffling winds from the east
like the wailing orchestra of orphans
like a city under water, moonless

Cry
for the absence of music
for the spilt milk
for the herniated disc along the border
for its water

Cry
when she cries
when she cries
Cry

Howl
for the ghetto girls
for the bass in your face
for January 6th pardons
for strange fruit

for boycotted fruit
for books

Howl
as you die
as you die
Howl

To the new administration
pick a nation
Bitcoin buys me pupusas
but don't come here
we'll send your ass back
put the beast on reverse
coffins on high demand
pipelines shut down
sacred land spared, for now

Cry
Into the river
Howl
Between the mountains cleavage
Into the dead eyes of lonely streets

Howl, Cry
On the perfect canvas of oil paint
Take the spirit of the steed
Shoot your bullets up to the clouds
Morph them into stretched veins

II

Ain't no big thing
Nationwide shortage of
Chicken wings

Someone is crying into the phone of gluttony

III

Cry,
For the smell of age
Howl
& blot out my rebellion

IV

My skin tags play a game of
hide and seek when I sleep
My nose bleeds when
I get horny and fussy
I drip poets into the drain of murals
Into the drain of obscurity

V

Cry, Howl

I still love the way your voice spreads like cream
When the hummingbird sucks on spoiled nectar
& how the earth is crashing down into a merlot hue
while Whitey sits on the moon
& I don't know why
We mistook our tears for water

Howl
as we climb the tree that thrives on loneliness
Cry
when we get to the top and find a rope

VI

Cry,
When you don't make it

Howl,
Where all the dead lie
Make a revolution with fire and blood
Especially if the dead are
children

Race you to the light

There is no light in the room
Children run but don't play
Their hands are torn and bleeding from racing to chain links
The doors open that's when the light comes in

Forgetting the sound of mamás voice
People come and go with more clothes on
It is winter, the season of separation
The light disappears into their designer scarves
We disappear into our aluminum blankets

One does not need to know a language
To know when they're being spoken of
One does not need to know a person
to read their eyes, some say "I'm sorry"
Some say, "What's for lunch?"
Time is different for others

Some children have a town in their eyes
Some a piece of fruit, some are still searching for a toy
Promised to them for keeping quiet,
They're the ones that hold the entire universe

Corre hacia la luz

No hay luz en la habitación
Los niños corren pero no juegan
Sus manos están desgarradas y sangrando, corriendo hacia los
eslabones de la cadena
Las puertas se abren, ahí es cuando entra la luz

Olvidando el sonido de la voz de mamá
La gente va y viene con más ropa puesta
Sombreros y guantes y café y sonrisas
La luz desaparece en sus bufandas
Así es como se dan cuenta que la temporada ha cambiado

Uno no necesita saber un idioma
Para saber cuando hablan de ellos
No se necesita conocer a una persona
para leer sus ojos, algunos dicen "lo siento"
Algunos dicen: "¿Qué hay para almorzar?"
El tiempo es diferente para otros

Algunos niños tienen el pueblo en sus ojos
Algunos una pieza de fruta, algunos todavía están buscando un juguete
prometidos si guardan silencio
Ellos son los que sostienen el universo entero

Through the Fence
for all immigrants

I offer these medicine poems
I gather this sage for you poems
Teach me to pray the rosary poems
Let's face the four directions together poems
In lak'ech- tu eres mi otro yo poems
Sweat together poems
Eres mi Yemaya poems
Flor Y Canto Poems
Don't drown in the river poems
Altar for our ancestor poems
sobadora curandera poems
Sana sana colita de rana poems
Drum beat poems
Conch shell poems
Cumbia poems y salsa poems
Hold my hand through the fence poems
Here's some food for your journey poems
La Bestia at high speeds poems
You are my kindred poems

Bring me your Dreamer poems
Your fuck this borderwall poems
Don't worry about the orange guy poems
Don't speak his name poems
Your existence is medicine poems
Help me uncelebrated Cinco de Mayo poems
ya basta! Poems
Grito poems
Indigenous wisdom poems
Palo Santo poems
You were here first poems

Decolonize your soul poems
Code-switch poems
You belong poems
No more war poems
Son Jarocho poems de Resistencia
Corrido poems
Con safos poems
Flying chancla poems

Share this meal with me poems
Here! Drink some water poems
Let me die your death poems
One day at a time poems
Café con leche poems
Pan dulce poems
Pupusa poems
Guayaba poems
Mangüitos con alguashte poems
Raspa poems
Espiropapa poems
Platanitos poems
La Pulga poems
Molcajete poems

Pocho poems
Salvi poems
East L.A. poems
Valle poems

Gather in this embrace poems
Crying poems
We're waiting for you on this side poems
We have hot coffee and tamales poems
Recipe poems
Share my rebozo poems
Come, fall in love poems
You are worth more than any labor you do poems

17

You are him, her, they, them poems
Welcome home poems
Get some rest poems
Tomorrow we'll plan the future poems
I love you poems.

Take with you these love poems
You are not illegal poems
We'll protect your women and children poems
You are not an alien poems
This is actually your land poems
You deserve so much more poems
Hide behind me poems
You are not merchandise to be locked up poems
Warsan Shire home poems
Como la flor poems
Tanto amor poems
La Llorona poems
Elotero poems
Be my chola poems
Pan de polvo poems
Orale vato poems
Slow dance poems
Padrino de DJ poems
Kiss me when I'm asleep poems
Deep tongue poems
Wildflower poems
Riversedge poems
Chicharra poems
First
&
Last
Breath
Poems
Stay speaking Spanish, it is poetry

*Poem for Resistencia en la frontera: Poets Against Border Walls

Por la Cerca

para todos los inmigrantes
traducido por Gabriella Gutiérrez y Muhs

Ofrezco estos poemas como remedios
Poemas recojo esta sabia para ustedes
Poemas enséñenme a rezar el rosario
Poemas enfrentemos a las cuatro direcciones juntos
Poemas En lak'ech—tú eres mi otro yo
Poemas sudemos juntos
Poemas Eres mi Yemaya
Poemas Flor y Canto
Poemas no se ahoguen en el río
Poemas altar para nuestros ancestros
Poemas sobadora curandera
Poemas sana sana colita de rana
Poemas de ritmo de tambor
Poemas de caracola
Poemas de cumbia y poemas de salsa
Poemas de agarra mi mano atravesando la cerca
Poemas de aquí tienes dinero para tu viaje
Poemas de la Bestia a velocidad alta
Ustedes son mis poemas afines

Tráeme tus poemas de "Soñadores"
Poemas de a la chingada con este muro fronterizo
Poemas de no te preocupes por el tipo anaranjado
Poemas de no digas su nombre
Poemas de tu existencia es remedio
Poemas de ayúdame a no celebrar el Cinco de Mayo
Poemas de ya basta!
Poemas de Grito
Poemas de sabiduría indígena
Poemas de Palo Santo
Poemas de que tu llegaste aquí primero
Poemas que decolonizan tu alma

Poemas de "code-switching" *
Poemas de "perteneces"
Poemas de "no más guerra"
Poemas de Resistencia Son Jarocho
Poemas de Corridos
Poemas con safos
Poemas de chancla voladora

Poemas de "comparte esta comida conmigo"
Poemas de "tómate agua"
Poemas de "déjame morir tu muerte"
Poemas de "un día a la vez"
Poemas de café con leche
Poemas de pan dulce
Poemas de pupusas
Poemas de guayaba
Poemas de manguitos con alguashte
Poemas de raspa
Poemas de platanitos
Poemas de La Pulga
Poemas de molcajete

Poemas pochos
Poemas de Salvi **
Poemas de East L.A.
Poemas del Valle

Poemas juntémonos en este abrazo
Poemas llorando
Poemas de "te esperamos en este lado"
Poemas de "tenemos café caliente y tamales"
Poemas de receta
Poemas de "compartamos mi rebozo"
Poemas de "ven, enamórate"
Poemas de "vales más que cualquier labor que desempeñes"
Poemas de "eres él, ella, ellos"
Poemas de "bienvenido a casa"
Poemas de "descansa"
Poemas de "mañana planeamos el futuro"
Poemas de "te amo."

Poemas de "llévate contigo estos poemas de amor"
Poemas de "no eres ilegal"
Poemas de "protegeremos a tu mujer y tus hijos"
Poemas de "no eres un extraterrestre"
Poemas de "esta es actualmente tu tierra"
Poemas de "mereces tanto más"
Poemas de "escóndanse detrás de mí"
Poemas de "No eres mercancía para que te encierren"
Poemas de casa de la poeta Warsan Shire
Poemas de "Como la flor"
Poemas de "tanto amor"
Poemas de "La Llorona"
Poemas del elotero
Poemas de "sé mi chola"
Poemas de pan de polvo
Poemas de órale vato
Poemas de baile despacito
Poemas de Padrino del DJ
Poemas de "bésame cuando duerma"
Poemas de lengua profunda
Poemas de flores silvestres
Poemas de la orilla del río
Poemas de la chicharra
Poemas
Del
Primer
Y
Del
Último
Respiro
Sigue hablando español, es poesía

Poema de Resistencia en la frontera: Poetas Contra el Muro Fronterizo

* en una nota "cambio de código en el lenguaje, o sea hablar en inglés
y español simultáneamente.

** Salvi- salvadoreñx/a/o; de El Salvador

When a City Ends

I

a poor kid sees clean clear water
he envisions a treasure, a hope
have you ever seen a murky
opaque wishing well?

II

When a woman kneels
along the river's edge to wash her sheets,
she thinks, a new beginning, a cleansing,
When was the last time you washed your clothes in oil?

III

When a thirsty stray dog walks for miles
along the gutters of this nation
wishing to quench her thirst
Where does she find relief?

IV

When have you seen
dogs or cats, blood dripping
from their jaw hair
laying on your front porch content?

It happens, blood and oil mix with mother earth's tears, and
we watch as it happens.

V

Soon we'll be drenched.

VI

question marks fall from trees in place of leaves, a girl yells at me
saying her dog has down syndrome and that I should believe her
like I believe in last night's moon, "even if he does" I cry, I worry
about being bitten. When a city ends, poems get shorter, sometimes
just a word long. We stay away from windows, and breathe slowly
in anticipation of, what, the end? People loot and turn mad, while
others pull flowers out of the rubble, sometimes finding the missing
not meant to be found. They hear a loud voice coming from the
North, sounds of wailing drums, the sound of a faint condolence,
like gasps.

VII

the earth sneezes, snores, and coughs, and you feel like grabbing
the priest from his collar and demanding an answer. You sleep with
jeans and tennis shoes on in case you need to run out of your home,
in the silence of night you hear the cries and howls and sirens. You
hear death. You see nothing. Normalcy is replaced with eeriness and
the moon wears down on you something heavy. You want to sleep,
but the earth starts to tremble again. Your past due bills are forgiven
until everything is back to normal, then you return to the purple of
days.

VIII

I do yard work and get all sweaty. I wait for the smell to set in. I
splash some old spice and I'm the old you. Armpits and cologne. I
walk around smiling and on my tip-e-toes to make myself tall like
you, I call out for the cenzontle that flew away the day you died.
I drink coffee and watch black and white movies. I imagine the
woman in my home old and fraile, I tell her to cuss me out, because
today I am you, and I'm man enough to take it.

IX

I buy a stack of postcards with tacuazín having seizures: cure them
with short poems, send them to prison inmates doing time for

resisting the oligarchies of the world. Boil a beef shank and discard the meat, suck out the marrow while watching a soccer match between Everton and Manchester United. Go up on the roof and count passing cars with low tire pressure and engine trouble. Empty your pockets and put contents in a ziplock bag, if you have a box of cigarettes, smoke two at a time until your tongue gets scratchy, then proceed to lick a cat. Watch the evening news and scream "Lies, Lies, Lies" until the national anthem comes on. Write a lullaby or ode to your neighbor. Drink warm milk. Close your eyes. Count your breaths. Call me in the morning. This is how I cure the insomniac.

X

my memory returns, I'm twelve again. I am in love with a cinnamon skin colored girl who spends her day washing clothes in a light blue painted pila under a cloudless sky. I write poems to her every night in her native tongue that she can't decipher, so I draw hearts and balloons, stick figure animals and little children holding hands. I don't recall hurricanes or politics at that age, life was better in that third world country. At one time in my life only the adults died in my life, we just went missing. Music was life, the anthem of my youth was filled with bass drums and the introduction of raging resistance raps, when I couldn't move I listened to 80s love songs. I wrote more love poems, this time to Julia Roberts and Drew Barrymore and Wonder Woman. I was Erik Estrada on a motorcycle, with a gun, without violence, with a big smile, with straight teeth, with a badge that took down the maliantes, with an accent on this side of the border, on a television set, in a make believe world. I fear nothing when my memory returns. My mom is young and dyes her hair a color not to hide greys, but because she still feels beautiful enough to bring out the green in her eyes. I am fifteen again, the earth shakes and I ask God to forgive me for the first time.

FukcDumb

Get outta the way
Outta the moon
Get outta the alley
Outta the world

Get into a fight
Deep inside a wall
Get into a page
Deep inside a book

Grow some money
Spend it on your time
Grow some kids
Raise them to love

Drive into a hotel
Order some holes
Drive into the street
& paint them in blues

Bread and Circuses

*We are under the treatment: "bread and circus" (now less
bread and more circus).*

— MARÍA ALICIA DE LÓPEZ ANDREU, BUSINESSWOMAN

when you start paying attention
you notice, you're sitting
anchored by what's on the eye

there are car chases, explosions
missing children, epidemics,
drug busts, hollywood romances,
food shows, big pharma, royal theatre

politicians selling the usual, morning
news, primetime news, evening
news, all disappointment

no more eating out, food is delivered
from your favorite restaurant: wings,
burgers, sushi, tacos, salads, ice cream,
even coffee and donuts

Alcohol is coming soon. Wait! It's already here!

Televisions are over 80 inches
With surround sound
No need to go to the movie theatre
Everything you need is at home
No malls to leave home for either
The internet delivers
Exercise? without moving a few feet
In front of the tube
As you lose weight, commercials

Telling you, "You may have a condition"
"Take a pill that may cause a side effect"

Are you the ringleader? Or the clown?
When did we allow for tragedy and violence
as entertainment into our lives?Poemas que decolonizan tu alma

Pan y circo

Estamos bajo el tratamiento: "pan y circo" (ahora menos pan y más circo).

— MARÍA ALICIA DE LÓPEZ ANDREU, EMPRESARIA

cuando empiezas a prestar atención
te das cuenta, estás sentado
anclada por lo que está en el ojo

hay persecuciones de autos, explosiones
niños desaparecidos, epidemias,
redada de drogas, romances de hollywood,
espectáculos gastronómicos, grandes farmacéuticas, teatro real

políticos vendiendo lo habitual, por la mañana
noticias, noticias en horario estelar, noticias
de la noche, toda decepción

no más salir a cenar, la comida se entrega
de tu restaurante favorito: alitas,
hamburguesas, sushi, tacos, ensaladas, helados,
incluso café y donas

El alcohol llegará pronto. ¡Espera! ¡Ya está aquí!

Los televisores miden más de 80 pulgadas
Con sonido envolvente
No es necesario ir al cine
Todo lo que necesitas está en casa.
No hay centros comerciales para salir de casa
Internet ofrece
¿Ejercicio? sin moverse unos metros
Frente a la tele
A medida que pierdes peso, los comerciales

Diciéndonos: "Es posible que tenga una afección"
"Tome una pastilla que pueda causar un efecto secundario"

¿Eres el jefe? ¿O el payaso?

¿Cuándo permitimos la tragedia y la violencia
como entretenimiento en nuestras vidas?

Clowns in the Valley

A circus clown invited another clown down here to the Rio Grande Valley to look at a wall. A pair of dunces watching an unfinished wall.

Then I took a photo and short video of a butterfly that crossed over that same border to play amongst our sunflowers.

The circus will continue with or without these clowns, new clowns will take their place, only the makeup will change.

The butterflies will slowly stop coming, they will disappear because the clowns are too caught up in getting cheers and applause and not what goes on around them.

Every once in a while the tiger's cage will come unfastened and eat a clown or two, but they will be replaced and the tiger will be put down, and they will add extra security and locks to the cages.

And the circus goers will eat cotton candy and peanuts and drink large coca colas.

When the circus turns off its lights, the clowns remove their makeup, smoke cigarettes, and drink whiskey. They will gamble with the money they made from all the entertainment and do it all over again the next day, and the next, and forever.

Let's send our VP to Guatemala!

They will come clothed as fragrance
They will come asking for kisses
They will come asking for a bowl of ants

They will drink all the rain water you've saved
for the drought filled summers
They will peel the mangoes and leave
the skins for the opossums to feed
on when everyone is dreaming

They will come with fog
They will come with death
They will come when you're the happiest

They will come when you're putting on your socks
They will come running into your arms

As an open wound
In clots
Unstitched
To avenge the past
Just to make you suffer some more
Oh how you'll suffer!

You'll run into the rivers
Hands spread open
wide eyed and hopeful

You'll fly into the cages
You'll be clothed in aluminum
You'll mourn the sun
You'll still hear the churning of the beast
You'll hit a wall

Concrete to the face
Smashing your dreams

Making you hate your language and religion
Making you regret
You ever wanted to trade
Suffering and death
For hope

At least suffering and hate
Invested in you
Hope never planned on opening its door

Pandemic Phlegm

A year in gridlock
Stuck, like trying to run in a dream
Paralyzed, a year long congestion of the soul

I dreamed I kept punching a 45-year-old man
And his face was bloody and my fists were raw
But my knuckles still had layers of struggle I had to remove
But the blood flowed like molasses and my hands weighed as if
I were holding up an ocean and all its existence

Being awake was no different
A pandemic phlegm
a glimpse of defeat
a screaming lining of
unanswered prayers to
a god that has abandoned
my calls late at night
still counting to a million

We see people in line at the coagulated supermarkets
Their lipmasks moving and grunting complaints
Making life and death political
Making politics about life and death
In Wisconsin 500 vaccines are left out to spoil
In hospitals blood oxygen levels drop
In restaurants employees never knew lockdowns
So many dead, no funerals to attend, no flowers
No memory of last breaths, dying in solace,
What road does death drift towards when no one is around?

Poets are writing poems between cries and quiet coughs
With delicate spiritlike care, with sufferin' singin'

Where they land
May they heal
May they heal
May they heal
Wherever they may land

Canto Fronterizo

I

Oh river, why do you weep
I see you flow
I see you flow

Oh river, when do you sleep
I hear you moan
I hear you moan

Oh river, why are you red
I see your body
I see your body

Oh river, why are you lost
I see you run
I see you run

Oh river, how can I help
Show me your hands
Show me your hands

Oh river, show me your heart
Grab on to the wind
Grab on to the wind

II

Rio Grande
Return our dead
Start with the rocks in your belly

Rio Grande
Return our dead
First the children then the birds

Rio Grande
Return our dead
The tresses of mamá

Rio Grande
Return our dead
The gold tooth of papá

Rio Grande
Return our dead

III

Tell me rain
Did you feel abandoned

Tell me rain
Did you hear voices

Tell me rain
Did the wind take you to dry land

Tell me rain
What cloud pushed you off

Tell me rain
What wandering song made you cry

IV

Border poet
Why did you stop writing

V

Keep your eyes on the children
Keep your eyes on the children

VI

Ay tierra, que tan grande es tu dolor
Será la lluvia el sonido de tu llanto

Ay tierra, que tan grande es tu llanto
Será el viento el susurro de tu dolor

VII

Cielo azul, dónde se escondieron tus nubes, la cobija de mi tierra,
hace calor, y los niños piden sombra

Cielo negro, donde esta mi luna, dos pájaros cantan su amor, y no se
encuentran en esta oscuridad

Cielo gris, ayudame encontrar mi sombra, se fue con mi amor, en sus
manos, un quetzal y las llaves de mi casa

VIII

Dónde están los niños
Donde estan
Donde

IX

It's not that the flowers don't bloom
They are dreaming

I know the road to you
I'm just waiting for my horse to finish drinking water

It's not the wind speaking
It's the water wading and slicing through the tendrils of the earth's
tresses, the voice comes from the water, the wind is mute

I know the scent of hyacinth
Their dead are scattered across the land taking last breaths, leaving its
blue song to struggle alone

X

Come here!
Pray with me

Come here!
Sit with me

Come here!
Hold on to me

Come here!
Sing with me

Come here!
Wish with me

Come here!
Dance with me

Come here!
Grow old with me

Come here!
Run with me

Come here!
Breathe with me

Come here!
Bleed with me

Come here!
Don't let me die alone

After we choke

and the virus leaves us, we return to the riversong

When I think of our river
I don't see boats
It's not a body of water either

More like blood
Like a swirl of intestines
Shoes without laces

Strings and beads of
Scapular and Rosary

No water
Not our river
More like blood

Like a distant song
A lone guitar strum
A floating tombstone

The looming branches of the anacua
Take pity on this floating spine

Not a river
Not a river at all

More like a drool

The Hemmingway

I don't want to go out the Hemingway,
way out of this world
Away from the fish I'm yet to catch

Fish out of sea, see out of this world
without mastering the art of kissing,
kiss
        kiss
                kiss away art,
you see?

Who will tell the stories that only I can?
Cuentos, the bloody ones,
the ones hiding on the edge of death's lips,
the bloody and bleeding,
cantos de sangre,
        sagrado corazon,
                sangre con cuentos

Blood trails inside
the stomach of the hanging tree
have a voice,
voices of rotting fruit, of
        Prison poems
                of   20th Century riots   of
                                    trigger happy cops

        But let's talk about the moon

           La luna, moonshine,
        moonlight, light of the cachetona,
      fisgona, chismosa luna, gossiping moon,
    mentirosa in solstice, who will uncover her true light
           if i go out the Hemingway?

A
Witness to dream-crossers
Poetas with riverbacks, never wetbacks, only setbacks,
always wading in water,
                waiting in compact spaces
for the chota to drive away,
                                away,
                                        a güey,
                                            ay güey!,
                                                Go
                                                    away!

But not the Hemingway.

Who will uncover the abortion of the sun?
The love song? The kissing deep-tongue?
Lengua en la garganta de la separada,
                                separate buttogether

Throatsong con-saliva
                        sin-saliva juntos
Callejón cojidas,
                cojer en callejones,

apagando los cellfones, en vibrate
                                Vibrando,
                                        vibing and
                                becoming the sun

In a dark alley,

I need to stay, the Hemingway stay,

Depressed, stressed, undressed, caressed,
cuerpo de oso,
                Oh   so
                        close,
But who will tell on the oligarchy? Who will bleed on paper?

Sangre, angry, lucha de lucha de lechuza,
                              su lucha,
                                        la lucha, la leche
Leche de vaca, el gobierno es caca, máscara, masquerade,
Massacre, mamadas, montañas, Tony Montana,
Say hello to my little

Code-switch stories,
                    switchcode cuentos,

duende, who will foster my duende when i'm gone?
Duende huérfano sin familia, orphaned keys

                                        &
                                                orphaned pennies
& orphaned poets y taquitos de muertitos
        Near evergreen cemetery, where we laid our street to rest
In peace, in pieces, pedazos, plomazos, balazos, stray bullet number 9

                        I don't
                I don't own a gun!
            I don't want to be blamed!
            I don't want to be your terrorist!
        I don't want to be your brown. man. killer. poster. child.
    I don't want you to break down the door to my sacred space.
I don't want to be in a documentary on the anniversary of my death
                    & your death
                    and their deaths.

        Keep your guns away from me, far away
                Put them to rest

            The Hemmingway

43

Autumn 2016

The little girl with amber hair first came to me in the fall of 1989. She sat with her back against me not too far from the pile of fire ants that aggravated me every day. I remember she had this large pink bow in her hair, Mary Jane shoes, and a small plush doll that always rested between her right underarm. She was an only child. Her parents were separated by alcohol and domestic violence and finally... too many sleeping pills. She lived with her grandmother in the house that sits on one and a half acres, about twenty skips away, if you have long legs. Something about trees that humans find good use for, piñatas on birthdays, a large tire for swinging, carving out their love's initials, sticking fire crackers in my tiny holes, climbing (which I don't mind at all) and like the young girl, someone to cry and speak to.

Just about a foot away lies buried the family dog. He was old and sick and was put to sleep. She cried and visited him often. I saw her grow and she stayed loyal to me. Especially in the fall. This is when she laid near me on a blanket and stared at the sky for what seemed like hours and hours. She cried and wrote in a journal and had her first kiss on the other side of me, where the woodpecker left a decent hole for her to stick notes in. She was only 16 in the autumn month of November when she had her first kiss. The boy was afraid and so was she. He had tamed hair, black, with a sharp chin and brown skin. Her eyes were like my leaves, an orange and light brown hue of early December.

I never saw much of the rest of the family, they gathered in the living room and kitchen, or sat up front with the ash trees. There, the squirrels chased each other for long sessions and all I could hear were the rustling of leaves and branches and the occasional giggle from the adults smoking marijuana, and listening to Tejano music. She was the only friend to my looming branches that gave the impression of wanting to be grabbed and broken off. She didn't do that though, she caressed my leaves and appreciated my shade.

44

Late September of 2016, she came to me at 3am. I felt something graze my branches several times before I felt a pull and a nervous hurrying motion. Then a long weight came down on me. God blinded me. All I could do was make out muffled sounds. In the morning the sun's heat put me to sleep. Over the years I have discovered that that is what happens to us when human tragedy and nature come together.

Her name was Autumn.

I Return to Love L.A.

We landed on time. The pavement outside
the small airplane window was wet, and from where I sat
I could almost smell the petrichor
settling in
on la la land.

I've missed my city, a mourning at times
The smog   The homelessness   The crime
The struggle, All of it!
The cholos and cholas   The low riders
Whittier Boulevard,
City Hall and all its suited criminals,
the immigrant culture, the graffiti,
the ghetto bird, the flat foots, the taggers, the *pinche* traffic jams,
the murals, the scent of gunpowder... sadly, *hasta eso!*
the second I step foot
the streets gave me the *chisme*,
on the corner of hustle

I saw raw courage and fight in a school teacher
holding up a strike sign! Oh yeah! She was like
the Statue of Liberty, like a Virgencita Guadalupana,
como una flor, la Emma González, la Alexandria Ocasio-Cortez, asi mero!
She smiled for my camera and continued her grito,
on the corner of Mission and Yellow Caution Tape Boulevard

My mother, hit seventy years of age
and still dances on Wednesday afternoon,
my chiquita viejita, always busy, still making
the best coffee and desayunos, I stare at her
watching a soccer match on television,
I can almost feel my dad next to her,
he left his costumbres for her to carry,

46

she misses him,
the flat on Gabriel Garcia Marquez knows it
Some things have changed and some stay the same:
They've moved my gente con gentrification,
the mariachis are still hustling on Boyle
strumming and tuning their guitarrones,
the borrachitos are still stumbling in and out
of the bar with the velvet curtain
except it's now a puerta de madera,
there on la calle primera

On the corner of shank and choke
Are the huddled men that lost hope
Fists closed around a bottle of memory
Glossy eyes not to be mistaken with tear welling eyes,
glossy... like distance.
The fathers of the barrio, the forgotten ones,
the addicted ones, the lost ones across Hollenbeck Lake

Across from wounds and addiction
Are the women that were robbed
Hair chopped short with blue-veined breasts that leak earthmilk,
long fingernails to climb and detach tomorrow's suicides,
the women of wounds, raising children,
goddamned children of the barrios, birthing more
children in safe zones, trying to rush into
menopause and divorce, slicing the bully in
the gut, breaking away from the man, breaking away
from the plan that the man can with no plan.

I return to love L.A.
Introduce her to my daughter
Who's hazel eyes are like a California sunset,
who's skin is bronze by ancestral blessings,
who's voice code switches with the morning whistling
of Santa Ana winds, who's morning yawn stretches
from Tejas to el Centro de Los Ángeles

I return and love my L.A.
with a new set of eyes, translating poems in
the shape of birds on power lines and river water
under the bridge, on the tracks,
where boxed cars wait to be pushed across the country,
Where homeless women push
shopping carts filled with garbage stanzas,
leaving poems in my mother's palms,
where palm trees sway with morning traffic,
I throw my city poems out the window
driving on the 5 and pause to breathe
on the 10 heading west

Until I return, I will hold my breath
I will hold it long enough
To remember
I never left

When Will The World Mourn Together

No death deserves an asterisk
No death deserves intent
No death deserves hate
No death deserves forgetting
No death deserves celebration

All lives deserve a full ride
Without an obstacle of hate
Without permission to breathe
Without permission to speak
Without permission to love
Love, anyone

When will we mourn together?
When news breaks that
One of our own has died
A death that questions
Our own faith and purpose
that makes us question who we can trust

When will we search together?
For a new way to walk through
This life with a joyful end and meaning
For all, ALL

When will you empathize with heartbreak
When will you pick up a dead bird and give it a resting space
When will you smile and hand a few coins to the homeless
When will you forgive yourself for hurting YOU

A long cry is necessary
For all, draining that sorrow
The one that turns into a dark

River inside of us, LET IT OUT!
Let it run through you

Don't accept details of death anymore
Don't accept breaking news anymore
Don't accept promises from politicians anymore
Don't accept promises from anyone anymore
Don't allow people with little know try to show
Don't allow a day to go by without feeling love
Don't allow a day go by without a heartfelt laugh
Don't allow a day to go by without being kind to yourself

Don't accept details anymore of death
Instead, ask that they tell you all the beauty they carried
Death is the finality of a life observed

We must learn to mourn together, for all, so we can
Learn to respect and love each other
In whatever shape, color, or beauty
Take this life on a ride
Think about that, hard

Ride this life, in your best outfit
Our bones are all the same
Our ashes, will blow

Children of maiz
Of red earth lullabies
Mud faced pequeñitos

Learning how to smile
Learning the alphabet

ABC, ICE, FBI, CBP, USA

River boys and girls
Desert children of wind

Cry
Cry
Cry

Children of Coatlicue
Shining children of the skies

Hold on
Hold on
Hold hands

ABCDEFGHIJKLMNOPQRSTUVWXYZ

Use these letters to tell your truth
Use these letters to tell your angst
Use them to change this world

I LOVE YOU

Children

Dry up the river, child
save your little sister

Send a deluge, child
your little brother is thirsty

Desertchild with cracked lips
Hear the rain coming

Riverchild with drowning lungs
Hear the song of the sun

Desertchild
look up
ask the stars to lead you
grab on to the prickly pear
eat away at the thorns
swallow the lizard king

Riverchild
reach for the mesquite branch
let the claws of the grackles
dig into your back
Lift, lift you to dry land

Separated children
stick together
memorize your language
keep singing your songs

Mamá y Papá are near
eat and drink and build strength
Remember abuelitas lullabies
and abuelitos stories

Mr. border patrol agent
Look into the eyes of the children
Look real good into their eyes
Do you see danger or hope?
(It's your reflection)

Mr. ICE agent
After you knock the door down
What's pointing at you?
A gun or a family in fear?
(Put your arms around it)

Mr. President
Abolish your hate
Abolish your fear
Abolish your ego

You!
Save the children
Save the children
Save
The
Children

Resisting the so-called "Patriots"

There is an unsettling odor
decay in our country

A great silence, too loud
sending shivers across souls

We activate our revolution
not loudly, steadily, we've been here before

we've been here before
we've been here before
we'll be here again, ready

Our elders are dying
We must lay them to rest, with respect

Our children are scared
We must reassure them, with honesty

We are faced with domestic danger
it's real, it takes two thumbs

There's an unsettling decay in our country
sending shivers across souls

With the force of the wailing redearth wombs
Ancestral cantos and contrails of protective sage smoke

We must lay them to rest, with our resistance
once and for all, and for good, with extra dirt

We have been here before, when we were stars and prayers
before our land became unsettled, before its decay

We are the children of Coatlicue and Floricanto
Resisting the so-called patriots and their disease

Rio Grande, Rio Bravo

I hear your whispers,
it's not the wind speaking anymore
it's your longing and your spirit
in the leaves, in the ripples, in the razor teeth of separation

Entre tierra mojada, the scent of mud
that brings me to you, the birdsong that makes its way to us from
across two lands that share the same language of the heart that brings
me to you

Rio Grande, Rio Bravo
the hope of a new people
the baptism of the new mestiza, nepantlera

We hear the echoes of pain and struggle and
the chants of "si de puede! y aquí nos quedamos"

Rio Grande, Rio Bravo

it's not the wind speaking anymore
it's the water

it's the water
it's not the wind speaking anymore

Rio Grande, Rio Bravo

we hear the echoes of pain and struggle and
the chants of "si de puede! y aquí nos quedamos"

the hope of a new people
the baptism of the new mestiza, nepantlera

Rio Grande, Rio Bravo

entre tierra mojada, the scent of mud
that brings me to you, the birdsong that makes its way to us from
across two lands that share the same language of the heart that brings
me to you,

it's not the wind speaking anymore
it's your longing and your spirit
in the leaves, in the ripples, in the razor teeth of separation

I hear your whispers

II. HOWL

"Terror melting into wonder, then slipping into peace."

— Father Greg Boyle

god as tree, tree as god

*"If the rumble of the remote
tree disturbs you
it is not for lack of concern."*
—Tezozomoc

I sometimes think god is in the trees
my tree especially, god is my tree

the birds that hover over His crown, angels
who bring petitions and offerings from the four directions

god, is the sun and moon to the ancestors
the eternal dreamers preparing the way

god, is the veins of mother earth
the roots, the rocks, the soil, the witness

I lay my hands on my god when I am fatigued
I lay my cheek on my god when I need an answer
I place my lips on my god when I am thankful
I sit at god's feet when I need a friend
I place my hands on my god when I'm losing faith

I sometimes think my god is in the trees
my tree, the trees I drive past, the trees on tv
burning by the thousands, the ones falling alone in the forest
the new ones being planted, uprooted

my god in the trees
breathing slowly, not complaining
breathing harder, transforming
breathing, liberating themselves from sin
breathing, unifying nature
breathing, for the resurrection

my god, my life, tree

When visiting the elders

Eating Chocolates in Silence

I wanted to hold hands with an 80 something year-old woman named Chuchis, but it was not my place and she couldn't say it was ok for me either way. So we sat together in silence for a while eating sugar free chocolates, and then I read the poem Oranges by Gary Soto to her. She smiled and I smiled, and continued eating chocolates in silence.

The 200 Year-Old Man

Jesus Dolores Perret Borrego, born in 1819, in a small ranch in Mexico called El Recuerdo. I told him to guess my age and he said sixty-one, I'm 46. He asked me if I believed he was two hundred years old, I smiled and before I could answer, he smiled and said, "No tengo porque mentir."

Mr. Perret has no wrinkles on his face, he is a living incorruptible, 200 year-old man waiting for an angel to take him home. His hands were large as we shook hands, he looked like a poet, born the year Walt Whitman was born, but in Mexico, in the small town of El Recuerdo.

Mary

Is ninety-two years old. The only black woman in the assisted living facility. Born in Victoria, Texas. I wanted to talk to her about music, and her life. Her voice had a smooth finish with each word. Mary had a table next to her with a cup of water and lipstick. I didn't ask the color, I want to say it was a soft brown from what I could tell when I glanced at her lips. She wore a perfect wig. She reminded me of Mary Wells, she asked me what kind of music I liked and what I did for a living. She beat me to the punch.

No time

No time to grieve for roses

When tree limbs hang after a storm
When barrio songs are tortured lullabies
When the virus is a political carrot dangling
When we still keep saviors nailed to a cross
When we still see humans hanging from trees

No time to lie to our daughters

Tell them at a young age, they will bleed
Tell them at a young age, they will bleed
Tell them, they can also leave a trail of blood for survival
Tell them, their voice is a nation

No time to watch

What others are creating
What others are loving

What others are
                    doing,
                            saying
                                    or destroying

Make time

to grieve for the dying
to grieve the last bloom

tzotzil

alfredo

alfredo sat on a concrete slab with his wife and son. they were all eating something from a styrofoam plate, pollo deshebrado and something else I couldn't make out. he was about five feet and some inches from what I could gather from my position next to him. he was prieto and looked like he was near sixty years of age. alfredo, one of the many asylum seekers along with his family, were taking a break from the noise of another restless afternoon. I told him he reminded me of my dad, quiet and humble. alfredo is forty years old, I am forty five.

carlos

sixteen and doesn't keep his eyes off his sister who is at a distance making a bracelet with a group of volunteers from brownsville, texas who come over to share their time and educational skills to bring hope to the children and young teens that live in the tent community of Matamoros, tamaulipas, mexico. he doesn't speak or make eye contact with me, he looks younger than sixteen.

angelina

She speaks in tzotzil only. she says a few words to her husband and he responds. Does she speak Spanish? no, he replies.

yesika

She never came back to her parents and brother while I was there, and she left her bracelet behind.

the age of softening

I see pictures of my mother
with silver hair, the age of softening

Is in her house now. Dad has gone,
she swallows the clouds that pass

Hoping to taste his sweat one last time
Hoping to taste his tears one last time

Mom, when did we grow up and forget
your cradling hands and sweet kisses?

I want to be that child again. I want to
be held in your arms snuggling with

My face buried in your neck, and feel your
Hands pat me to sleep. When did I forget

You worked jobs that had you hunched over
for hours at a time and still came home to

Clean up our mess? How many times
Did I tell you I Love you? Was it enough?

When I sleep, may my breaths
be odes of love for you.

I believe
after Blas De Otero

I believe in human beings. I have seen
children torn away from families, daughters
swaying from closets and ceilings, men face down
on gutters with blood trickling into sewers,
and I believe it.

I believe in peace, I have seen stars
shoot from one end of the sky to the other
side of heaven, planets go dark, and ashes
come down like rain, I have seen and I believe it.

I believe in you, my country. I will tell you
what I have seen: I have seen rivers run dry
with footprints the size of wallets and knives
with crimson songs, playgrounds with echoes
of children's laughter and rain that taste like
border tears; still my heart beats for more;
I have seen it
and I believe it.

Mama's Struggle

Mama always dressed for comfort.
The hardest part was getting undressed.

The tucking of large breasts into a cheaply
made bra that by the end of the day left deep

creases over her shoulders and along her sides.
Sometimes she would ask one of her sons to help

her with the strap and connect the little eye hooks.
Mama's body had scars.

A simple article of clothing: fabric, foam cups, sliders
rings, hooks, and underwires.

Mama never complained, she patted the cuts with
alcohol swabs and ointment.

Mama had one bra and many scars.

Capsized
a poem about alcoholism

I always thought of dad as an ocean
spume frothing from his mouth

mom would say tilt his head to one side
I pretended I controlled the sea

somewhere waves were created when I did that
so I looked at him and drew tiny boats on

his lips and cheeks, he moaned and groaned and I
pretended the sea was mad, so I drew

pirates on his chin, sometimes the sea would
gargle and toss back at me all the plastics and

garbage, pieces of sailors and forgotten
ships would emerge, one time he opened his eyes

and his green orbs flashed a mermaid
playing a violin, playing a song of longing

Volcado
un poema sobre el alcoholismo

Siempre pensé en papá como un océano echando
espuma de su boca

mamá decía muevele la cabeza hacia un lado Fingí
controlar el mar

en algún lugar se crearon ondas cuando hice eso así que lo
miré y dibujé pequeños botes en

sus labios y mejillas, se quejaba y quejaba y yo fingido que el
mar estaba loco, así que dibujé

piratas en su barbilla, a veces el mar
hacía gárgaras y tiraba todos los plásticos y

basura, pedazos de marineros y olvidados surgirían
barcos, una vez abrió los ojos
y sus orbes verdes destellaron una sirena
tocando un violín, tocando una canción de nostalgia

He lay on his back

searching for the stars, motionless

His mother bore him in a oval tub
with the help of a doula
en agua, sin medicine

The killer caused pain
to rain on her, como lluvia
like acid burning through her skin
seeing the other side of the street through his head

These are the stories of my youth,
dreams of death knocking on my door
sharpening her scythe, afilando
hasta que despierto con el olor de cuchillos
dandome los buenos días

They threw this kid through a window
Los Chuecos called it a suicido, we don't know suicide
suicide doesn't chase you up four flights, then out the window
suicide happens when it happens

He lay vertically on his back
searching, in the night's distance
but all he could see was the beginning
of a new rainstorm

They looked like stars for a moment
up there coagulating, like his blood
Forming a river, down the gutter

Origami

Intricate fingers
folding,
creasing

When making a cat
start with a 6 inch x 6 inch
grey square. All our cats
seem to be of the
tabby persuasion.

I ask my daughter,
What she wants for breakfast,
She shrugs,
folding,
creasing.
Her hair is up in a ponytail
She says her name is Safronia,
In the background Simone's
lyrics trail with the yelp from a
Paper
cut,
fold,
crease.

Tear another 6x6 inch square. Grey on one
half with cherry blossoms drawn on the other
half.
fold &
crease

my coffee cools as I stare out of the window,
thinking, "people used to burn in bed, people
smoked and burned in bed.

The coroner would come.
Unfolding the gurney,
Creasing the body bag

When bagging a body,
Start by making sure the area is taped off by
the screaming yellow caution tape and the
toe is tagged for identification.

fold,
crease,
crease,
fold,

On the table, another 6x6 inch
square, wavy designs in blues and whites, I
think of an ocean.
My coffee... cold now.

cut,
fold,
crease,
fold,
transforming,

Do you want eggplant? She asks

crease,
fold,
cut,

I stare out the window
thinking, some people don't smoke, but they
all die.

Blue Food Coloring
after Carolyn Forché's The Morning Baking

Come back, I forgot
my daughter wants to know,
if she took blue food-coloring,
how many drops would it take
for you to change your mind
about...wait! What's a
synonym for suicide?

Come back, I forgot
women can vote now
she's more than certain there's a law
that will protect you, or at least, for sure,
a Woman's group that will empower you
to leave him. Shall I help her little hands?
Raise you up, dust you off, brush your hair, and swarm
you with love and songs?

Come back, I forgot
black and white photographs don't
give the color of your eyes justice,
and no one talks about you anymore.
do they also drip hazel acrylic tears? Ours do.

Come back, I forgot
there's a thing about your hands,
my friends and I know that hands have
these lines that tell of a long or short life span.
I bet yours reached around to the front
of your index finger and right now
I can't breathe because you should've been here
for great grandma, she is nearing your light
but I'm afraid she forgot what you look like

Come back, she forgot
to say goodbye and I want
a picture of you both, maybe you could
be holding my grandma and three generations
can show your fourth that life happens
but giving up
changed our story.

Day one, Estate sale

Nothing is on discount
that's on Friday and Saturday
on Thursday, full price

Items we saw and bought and didn't buy:
a record of Perez Prado's greatest hits
adult diapers
silverware
2 hand painted birds from Tulum
Zippo lighters
a bag of Rosaries
a lamp
a desk
a bed
a heart-shaped mirror

I never see pillows
I never hear voices
They never tell the name of the deceased

I wipe my feet at the door
I enter each room with respect
if I touch anything, with care

Everything there was someone's all
I look at the things not for sale
the garden, window treatments
the trees, the neighbor's watching

I carry the birds of Tulum, one in each hand
and the neighbor across the street stops and stares
as if staring into a sunset
near some ruins
near a sinkhole

Four funerals

one.
she held a rosary in her
hands, between bruised
fingers and newly polished
nails across her chest

my *abuela* told me
"*esta bien hijo, tócala*"
she promised the fear of
the dead would leave my heart
forever if I touched her cold stiff hands

two.
right before they lowered
her 9 feet below, they snuck
his bones at her feet, the men
with rope handling gloves
dropped them both.
Everyone's bones shifted

three.
My surname belongs in a meat market
behind the swinging torso of cattle
to give the butcher hell
the first four letters never go on sale
because they are always alive
the last four fall off the scale
take a number and see if the
carnicero can roll his r's

four.
you pick my casket
I already picked my bones

My mother at the cemetery

I imagine my mother at the cemetery,
quiet and fumbling through words
abducted by the wind

She will be double-widowed in less than five years.
It is a wet day in summer
My father watches soccer in the living room.
My other father, I didn't know him, he must be holding on
to his kidney, delivering propane to a widow.

I imagine Lola at the nail salon,
Colorblind, taking in the smell of shellac
Picking a purple polish hoping she picked red
Tonight she has a date, the boy back home
Masturbates, on orders from the big brother
She hopes for a nice walk on the beach
He wants to bury her toes in the sand

I imagine Travieso at the liquor store
Twenty bucks in hand, two years too young
walking out with a Colt 45, stopped in his tracks
By a 45 Magnum, while 45 gives a speech about
Building a wall, & the barrio continues its
Slow walk and vibrating hymns six feet under
Walls don't stop bullets, I don't know of a 45 that ever did

I imagine my daughter walking to school
With orders, if the boys call you with grunts and whistles
Set them on fire, watch them ash, watch them fade
Then come back home, here, daddy will wash away the
Memory and replace your eyes with a set of new ones

In the cemetery

A tombstone — a sorrowful gray
there lies a poet
his only visitors — pigeons
the occasional writer with
a pad and pencil
conjuring inspiration from the grave
a child — the birthday flowers
& tears of remembrance
the friend — reads new poems
from an anthology of odes to rust

    Carved granite
    Slowly becoming a memory
    but did the poet not write about this?
    the grave — death — obscurities ?

The undertaker — listens
walks with a slow wither
that's what feeding grackles will do to pensive man
lost in his slow walk — like a stray bullet

    Mounds of marble — teeth of the city
    sinking into the gums of the earth
    cavities of silence
    the narrow lips of father
    the knuckles of abuelita
    the dead suit of abuelo
    the four winds of pandemia

In the cemetery:
Curtains — drawn down
everyday is a celebration of life

time passes — nothing changes
music comes in the form of footsteps and moans

flowers are pushed up for the living — flowers are pushed up, for our grief

Handkerchief

He holds a handkerchief to his lips
Mostly to catch the blood that bypassed the hole in his throat
Where blue lung sighs whispered pain
The cenzontle aches with each song
His grey suit folded on a chair next to his bed, prepared for its final fitting.
Abuelo smiles, coughs, & wipes his chin.

Abuelo smiles, coughs, & wipes his chin.
Before he dries his eyes from the pain that pushes out tears.
Always smiling through the longest fight for his life.
Grandma stirs the tea and hands it to him, then walks away with a broken spirit.
Abuelo smiles & reaches for her hand.
She trembles with each touch from his frail-fingered caress
She prays with anger and resistance.

She prays with anger and resistance.
Wears red lipstick that matches the floral design on her apron.
She puts away the calendar & goes to mass when the bells toll.
She dreams of this stage of love to be restful, blessed.
The cenzontle takes flight and returns three days later.

The cenzontle takes flight and returns three days later.
His song changes, it comes with a new accent.
The nights grow longer and the blood flows often.
Grandma has stopped making tea.
The suit drapes on a hanger.
Grandpa doesn't sleep through the night anymore.

Grandpa doesn't sleep through the night anymore.
The china is put away, except for two cups, one glass, a spoon, and a plate.
The watchman doesn't blow his whistle at night near grandpa's window.
People come and go, speaking in whispered tones.

People come and go, speaking in whispered tones.
Grandpa's breathing has slowed.
Grandma watches television on mute.
The cenzontle takes flight and returns the next day.

The cenzontle takes flight and returns the next day.
In beak, blood
& soil on its feet
My grandpa takes a long breath, looks into the sky, searching for his star
Holding a handkerchief to his lips.

Elegy for Vanessa Guillen

You disappeared in the spring, bluebonnet
They found you in the summer

robbed of your privacy
taken at the tender age of twenty

I never liked camouflage, but when
I see your photo on social media, the news
now on murals, I respect it, for you

A guerrera, una hija, a voice silenced

I go to my tool box
throw my hammer across the room
turn off the commercial with
4th of July advertisement
and hate camo again

You disappeared in the spring, sunflower
They found you in the summer

If we say your name enough times
Will you respond? maybe in the shrill
of the thirsty mockingbird in my garden

You are in the wind, like my father
like our friends taken in this pandemic,

O Specialist,
Dug deep with the lies,
America's daughter

You disappeared in the spring, lilac
You were found in the summer
Missing the dark skin of your ancestry

A secret unmasked by the thunder
of a mother in mourning of the riding voices
still chanting their echoes of justice

After the first death, there is no other
And yet, here we are again

You went missing in the spring, soldier
Your song was found in the summer

Maybe soon, they'll raise your
name to honor a school,
a park, a highway, an airport

Maybe sometime in spring
when flowers bloom wildly along
the highway, before another
dreaded Texas summerThe watchman doesn't blow his whistle at
night near grandpa's window.
People come and go, speaking in whispered tones.

There's a fireplace

An electrical one
Blaring
While my cats leg is amputated
A quiet violence under anesthesia

She lays, eyes open
Tongue tasting the air of
acepromazine and nickel

I'm listening to the veterinarian
While he shaves her down
I see a leg quarter
Like the one I put on my bar b que pit
& all of a sudden I'm contemplating
Becoming a vegetarian

I'm wiping the tears rolling down my face
Like the bingo disks on the Price is Right
One lands on my lips, another on my neck
One on my mustache
I ran her over with our car
I'm filled with guilt

A few years ago I nursed her to health
After she survived weeks of attacks from
the mockingbirds of Edinburg

She returned limp and thin
Her forehead bloody and scarred
Pecked away and lethargic
she filled into my arms
With hope and trust and hunger

Today, she sleeps
& will wake as a feline tripod
& will look around with eyes darting
at who to blame
I won't be there, I'll be here
Writing a poem of guilt

Love
for Lilly

In the garden
near the overlapping leaves
of the spaghetti squash and blackberries

A few feet away from the broken
bird bath that now holds the thriving coleus meant
for the perennial that once grew milkweed

But away from the thorns of the rose bushes

At 3am, by the pomegranate tree, but in silence to
let the butterflies sleep, covered in repellent,
never in regret, hands on the wood framed shed next to
the aging anacua tree, dropping drupes over our glistening shadows

Still, away from the eyes of the house

But always in the garden, barefoot with tiny insects having
sex between our toes while the moon drips milk into
our mouths and we grapple and twist and lock
arms legs and moan and uproot a new harvest opening
up & closing in a blink of an eye like the Night-blooming cereus

In the garden
A few feet away from the broken bird bath
Away from the thorns
At 3 am
Away from the eyes of the house
Barefoot

But always in the garden

A flag, when it burns

Is the fire sad?

How do you squeeze blood from a stone?

How do you console a longing?

What's a lament without rain?

My color is verdecito. Is that why hummingbirds land on my chest in my dreams?

My mother laughcries when remembering her past?

I dream in scar, in a blur, in greyness.

Today I smiled at a squirrel climbing a tree, frowned when a plane flew overhead.

Name a mountain.

The men of my youth would always ask if I was ready to visit with "the putas" then laugh at my reaction of nervousness.

A lizard crossed my path, a bullet for a throat, then it strayed off.

When did mental illness make the white privilege list?

I have a cigarette waiting to exhale.

St. Therese of Covid-19 Test Clinic on Primrose Avenue

How do you take care of a primrose? My thumb presses the search
tab. All the while wondering how this virus spreads. Maybe like
the primrose? Wildly, spreading in clumps wherever it may land.
My daughter laughs along with a friend while I fill out medical
information, she's nursing a fever and I'm thinking, "St. Therese"
probably the most special of all places right now for a miracle or at
least... a negative result. The lady returns in her protective gear and
a plastic bag containing a swab in one hand and a clipboard in the
other, "On a scale from 1-10 how uncomfortable is it, Dad?" She
asks. "Well let's skip 1-4" I say. The lady asks her not to move and to
lean back. I've been there for her first shots, dental visits, removal of
tonsils, scrapes, cuts, falls, and losses.

We drive off

I ask,
"scale of 1-10?"

"it hurt"

"it's real"

Later that evening, we watered our garden
Taking extra time on the area where the primrose
will grow, hopefully... wildly

Acknowledgements

"Blue Food Coloring" - Boundless 2018, anthology of the Rio Grande Valley International Poetry Festival

"Robbed At Knife-Point" - DRYLAND: A Literary Journal Based In South Central Los Angeles, *Pushcart prize nominee 2019*

"Mama's Struggle" - Interstice: creative journal of South Texas College

"Capsized" - The Big Windows Review *Pushcart prize nominee 2019*

"Canto Fronterizo II-IV" Grist a journal of the literary arts

"Through The Fence" - In Xóchitl, in Cuícatl: Floricanto, Cien años de poesía chicanx/latinx (1920-2020) - Editorial Polibea. Madrid, España

"Race you to the light" "Corre hacia la luz" and "Capsized" "Volcado" - Antología poética, Nuestramérica es un verso, antología poética 1968-1989

"Let's send our VP to Guatemala!" & "Cry, Howl" - REIMAGINE AMERICA: an anthology for the future - Vagabond

"Reason I don't own a gun" - Good Cop, Bad Cop: an anthology - FlowerSong Press

"Pandemic Phlegm" - ARTS ALIVE SAN ANTONIO

"Rio Grande, Rio Bravo" - CUTTHROAT, A Journal of the Arts Puro Chicanx Writers of the 21st Century, Opening poem for event, *In Memoriam Rio Grande*: A Protest against the Border Wall, May 26, 2019

"In the cemetery" - CUTTHROAT, A Journal of the Arts 15th Anniversary Issue 26, Summer 2021

To my family always, Liliana and Luisa Isabella
My support and love at every turn

A special thanks to Odilia Galván Rodríguez for believing in me and
supporting my work. To Priscilla "Lina" Suarez & Rodney Gomez
for all they do with our press to keep moving forward. To the entire
FlowerSong Press familia, gracias.

A special thanks to the Kindle Foundation Project for their grant
when things seemed to be tightening,
Houston Poetry Festival, Writers' League of Texas, The Philosophical
Society of Texas,
Texas Commission for the Arts, The Artist Foundation of San
Antonio, VASE, Region One, UT-RGV, and Dr. Enrique F.
Figueroa's GenteChicana/SOYmosChicanos **Arts Fund,** which is a
Donor Advised Fund at the Greater Milwaukee Foundation for their
generous grant as well.

And to my furry babies. All five of them. Whom one way or another,
have kept me company during my writing process.

About the Author

Edward Vidaurre is an award-winning poet. He is the 2018-2019 City of McAllen, Texas Poet Laureate, publisher & editor-in-chief of FlowerSong Press and its sister imprint Juventud Press. Vidaurre resides in McAllen, TX with his wife and daughter.

CPSIA information can be obtained
at www.ICGtesting.com
Printed in the USA
LVHW021519100222
710333LV00006B/124

9 781889 568096